D0636268

A PORTRAIT OF HULL

IAN CARSTAIRS

HALSGROVE

First published in Great Britain in 2006

Title page photograph: Pendant on the Lord Mayor of Kingston upon Hull's chain of office depicting the Armorial Escutcheon of the City Council.

British Library Cataloguing-in-Publication Data
A CIP record for this title is available from the British Library

ISBN 1 84114 538 6
ISBN 978 1 84114 538 9

HALSGROVE
Halsgrove House
Lower Moor Way
Tiverton, Devon EX16 6SS
Tel: 01884 243242
Fax: 01884 243325
email: sales@halsgrove.com
website: www.halsgrove.com

Printed and bound by D'Auria Industrie Grafiche Spa, Italy

Introduction

Be prepared for a big surprise. Hull, as Kingston upon Hull has been commonly known for hundreds of years, is a truly fascinating city whose virtues go largely unsung.

Viewed from the Yorkshire Wolds, or across the Humber Estuary from Lincolnshire, the limits of the city are broadly marked by the lofty Humber Bridge to the west and the pair of cooling-towers at Salt End chemical works in the east. Just beyond these modern structures stand two small historic buildings – a crushing mill, now missing its sails, and a tiny lighthouse – like quotation marks at either end of a long and interesting sentence. Between these landmarks lies perhaps one of the least known and visited cities in the country.

Over the years, I have travelled to Hull many times, though always to attend meetings. On each occasion, I would approach by the same routes, park in the same car parks and walk the same ways. Tackling *A Portrait of Hull* was a revelation. As I undertook my photographic expeditions I gained a wholly new perspective on the roads, squares and passageways and the buildings which lined them, especially the hugely-varied details of their upper façades which have endured, while the shop fronts at street level have changed in response to fashion and the economic fortunes of the businesses which occupy them.

Central to the quality of my experiences in the heart of the city was the decision to cast aside the car to travel in by bus using park-and-ride, and to explore everywhere on foot, freeing me from the shackles which navigating, getting lost, clock-watching over car-parking charges and all the other annoyances driving brings.

And rest assured, the variety of things to see within easy walking distance, spanning the city's bustling Queen Victoria Square to the freedom of the Humber waterfront and the Old Town with its delightful museums, is enough to completely absorb you.

I hope, like me, that you will find an enormous amount to discover or rediscover and to look at more carefully, prompted perhaps by this selection of photographs of things which caught my eye and held my attention. I certainly found that the harder I looked, the more I saw and the more I saw, the slower I walked and the longer I wanted to stay.

Ian Carstairs
2006

# Acknowledgements

Many people have helped me practically and with advice and information. Thanks is due to them all, notably staff at Hull City Council – Brian Hayton (Cultural Services); Simon Green (Museums and Galleries); Martin Taylor (City Archives); Hilary Byers (Planning/Conservation); Paul Stansfield (Kingston House); David Stipetic (Clock Custodian); Robin Diaper (Guildhall); Tony Ridley (City Hall); and Mike Lister (Hull New Theatre). Thanks is also due to Linda Martin, The Deep; The Rev Philip and Rev Marion Ball, Holy Trinity Church; Alison Harris and Captain Simon Walker, P&O; Bob Stones, Associated British Ports; Archer and Teresa Carstairs, Jan Knowlson and especially my good friend and photographic companion Patrick Ferguson. Thanks also to my editor, Roly Smith, Editorial Manager at Halsgrove, who, as ever, encouraged me throughout.

The photographs on pages 56 to 62 are reproduced by kind permission of the PPC of Holy Trinity Church, Kingston upon Hull; those on pages 29, 32–34, 67, 73–74, 82, 109–113, were taken by kind permission of Hull City Council Archives, Museums and Galleries.

Springtime in the city
Formal flower beds and fountains to the west of Queen's Gardens lift the spirits and set the scene for a visit to Hull.

A town is born

In 1293 King Edward I acquired the small port of Wyke at the mouth of the River Hull, renaming it Kingston (King's Town) upon Hull. The seal on the seven-hundred-year-old Charter of 1299, which established Hull as a self-governing community, depicts Edward seated. Unfortunately his head is missing.

History in his hands

City Archivist Martin Taylor (top left) holds the beautifully-illuminated Queen Mary I charter of 1553 (left), which refined privileges and jurisdictions within the Borough of Hull. The charters are held in the City Archives (above).

A new dawn
As the city sleeps, the aura from its street lights frames the spectacular Humber Bridge as first light creeps into the sky.

The edge of the ice
Before the last Ice Age, the coast lay close to where the Humber Bridge now stands. Viewed from the bridge, Clive Sullivan Way (named after an esteemed Rugby League player) sweeps below towards the city.

Park it
Just off Clive Sullivan Way, the Priory Park park-and-ride offers extensive free parking and a relaxing way to enter the city centre.

Opposite: **Strength in the wind**
The redundant mill on the foreshore by the Humber Bridge Country Park was once used for crushing the high-quality chalk from the nearby quarry for use in bread-making. When operational it was powered by unusual five-bladed sails.

KC Stadium
Set beside West Park, the 25,000-seat KC Stadium (named after its sponsors, Kingston Communications) is home to Hull City Football Club and Hull FC Rugby League Club, in addition to being a venue for major events and concerts.

Opposite: **A bridge so far**
The Humber Bridge is one of the longest single-span suspension bridges in the world and a superb and elegant example of modern engineering – its centre span is over three-quarters of a mile (1410m) wide. The best view of the bridge is gained from the end of the old docks near the St Andrew's Quay retail park.

Historic route

From the earliest times, the Humber has been an artery of water-borne trade, serving not only the communities along its lower reaches but also settlements upstream.

The fish docks
The William Wright Dock, seen here from a vantage point on the footbridge over Clive Sullivan Way, is the home of Hull's fishing trade, sadly now only a shadow of its former self.

The big drop
A special rig in Albert Dock is used to test lifeboats by dropping them into the water from a height similar to that of the deck level of ships.

Marking the way
Associated British Ports' aptly-named and specially fitted-out *Humber Sentinel* is used for setting and retrieving colour-coded buoys which mark channels and warn of dangers in the Humber.

Don't judge a book...
The utilitarian Paragon House (left) concealing the entrance to Paragon Street Railway Station, gives no clue as to the attractive space to be found inside the original Victorian structure completed in the late 1840s (above). However Paragon House will soon exist only in photographs when the new transport interchange is established.

Echo of the past
The entrance to the booking hall in Paragon Street Railway Station retains a traditional WH Smith station shop front.

ERECTED TO THE MEMORY
OF THE MEN OF
KINGSTON-UPON-HULL
WHO
LAID DOWN THEIR LIVES
FOR THEIR COUNTRY
IN
THE GREAT WAR
1914-1918
AND
THE WORLD WAR
1939-1945
THEIR NAME LIVETH FOR EVERMORE
ERECTED BY
PUBLIC SUBSCRIPTION
TO THE MEMORY OF
THE MEN OF HULL
WHO LOST THEIR
LIVES DURING THE
SOUTH AFRICAN WAR

Ever-changing
Nothing stands still. The new St Stephen's development under construction. Today's construction work delivers tomorrow's new buildings and demolition sites of the future. Ever has it been so.

Opposite: **Hull remembers**
The Boer War Memorial and the Cenotaph, set prominently in Paragon Square are poignant reminders of the cost of war, particularly in a city so heavily damaged as a result of bombing during the Second World War.

Small shops and big shops
Many small 'proper' shops, are found close into the city centre. Discovering them comes as a huge relief from the bland monotony of many city centres elsewhere in this country.

Covered cut-through
Paragon Arcade makes an interesting link between Carr Lane and Paragon Street, adding variety to the street scene.

High point
Kingston House, the tallest building in the city centre, offers a spectacular unobstructed vantage point to view Hull and its setting, as shown on pages 25 to 27.

The view south west
On the horizon lies the Humber Bridge. In the middle distance, the city landscape includes other tall buildings – the hospital and several blocks of flats.

Overleaf: **The view south east**
In this late afternoon view towards the sea (25 miles/40 kms away), the complex roofscape reveals some of the major buildings such as the Guildhall (with tower), Hull College (blue and white), court buildings (silvery domes), with the docks and Salt End chemical works beyond.

SHOTWELL
Danbys

Premier venue

With a 1400-seater auditorium and a huge traditional organ dominating the stage, the City Hall, completed in 1909, offers a grand concert and performance venue. Its design, along with that of neighbouring buildings, makes you wonder whether you are really in England.

A world-class instrument
Service lights inside the City Hall's organ create a dramatic silhouette (above). With more than 6000 pipes, ranging from vast boxes and tubes to curving ranks of tiny pipes (right), maintaining it is a major undertaking. The first recital on the organ was given in 1911.

Yorkshire Bank
sky

Opposite: **Heart of the city**
Queen Victoria Square, with its central statue of Queen Victoria, is the hub of Hull's shopping streets. The old Docks Office in the background is now the Maritime Museum.

City and sea
The Maritime Museum tells the story of Hull's proud association with the sea. Dominating the city centre, its architecture gives a continental flavour to a port which in past times tended to look outwards to overseas trade and making a living from the sea, rather than inland to other areas of England.

Yesterday's reality – today's heritage
The beautiful central staircase in the Maritime Museum (left) exhibits complex metal balusters. The courtroom is also spectacularly ornate (above).

Art at sea
The most significant collection in Europe of scrimshaw, the name given to the artworks of seafarers who engraved pictures into the teeth, bones and other parts of the animals which they hunted, is held in the Maritime Museum.

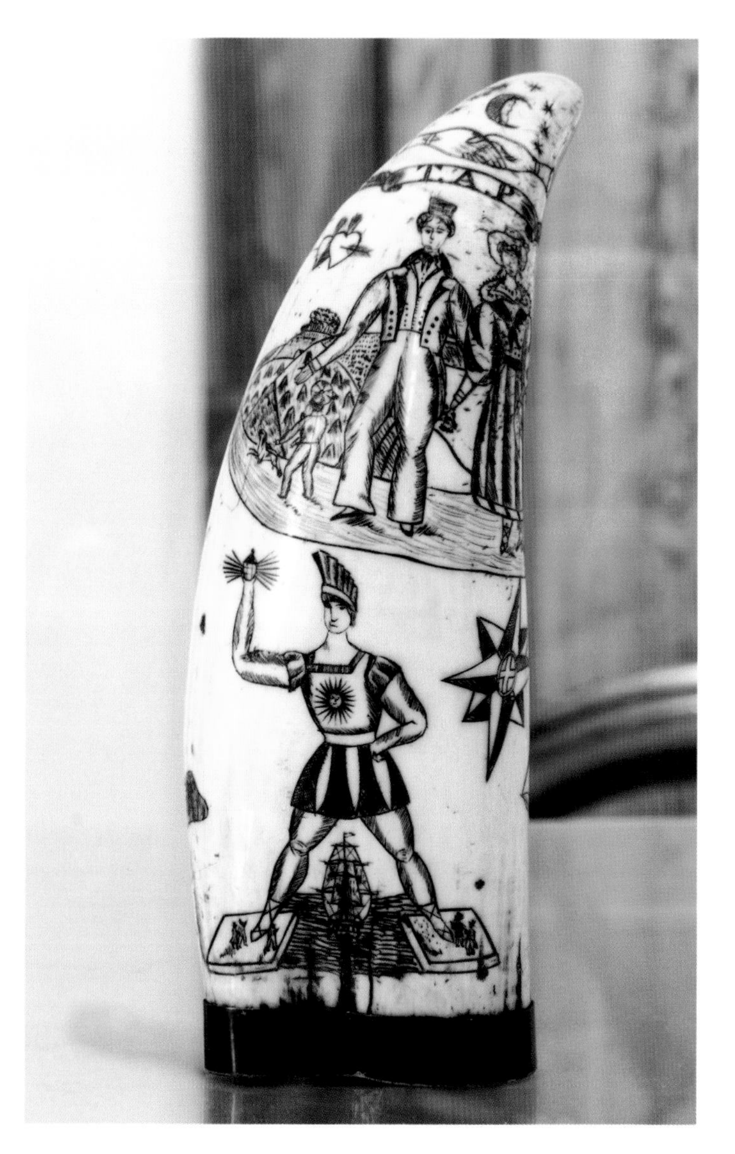

Changing times – different values

Today, whaling is banned by this country, but it was once an important industry, captured both in paintings and other collections of the tools of the whalers' trade. Shown here is the exhibit of an historic whaling boat (left) and a painting of a whaling expedition (above).

Maximum use of space
With radiating roads, wedge-shaped buildings fitting into tight corners are not unusual. The Yorkshire Bank adds its colourful contribution to Queen Victoria Square.

Elaborate details

Throughout Hull, pubs and hotels in particular sport surprising and complex designs and colours. The Punch Hotel (left), with its humorous depictions of Mr Punch set in the upper façade, and the building at Masters Bar on the corner of Paragon Street and South Street, could easily belong in fairytales.

Ferens Art gallery
A grey day transmutes the Ferens' contribution to Queen Victoria Square. With renowned international and national collections, the gallery is considered to be one of the finest regional galleries in the country.

Whitefriargate

Named after the Whitefriars – a Carmelite religious order which occupied land here in the Middle Ages – Whitefriargate leads into the heart of the Old Town. Lined by modern shop-fronts at street level, it retains widely different designs to the upper floors of the buildings.

Looking above eye-level
Examples of different architectural styles in Whitefriargate and Silver Street create a visual feast (here and overleaf).

Under the Act
Parliament Street is the most complete Georgian street in Hull, linking Whitefriargate and Alfred Gelder Street, and was built at the end of the eighteenth century following an Act of Parliament.

Land of Green Ginger
Hull's strangest and perhaps best-known street name (the origin is obscure) leads to a pleasing narrow street of old buildings, initially out of sight round a corner.

Preface to war
Tucked into an alleyway off Silver Street is the Olde White Harte public house, said to have been the place where Sir John Hotham, the then Governor of Hull, resolved to deny King Charles I entry to Hull in 1642, a key event at the start of the English Civil War.

Trinity House Lane
The prospect of Trinity Square beckons beyond the entrance to Trinity Market, Bob Carver's Fish and Chip Restaurant, and the Kingston Public House.

Opposite: **Long-term residents**
Trinity House covers the land of the Whitefriars' (Carmelites) Friary, dissolved by Henry VIII in 1539. The land was given to Trinity House in 1621, though the institution had been established in Hull since the fourteenth century. The main front shown here dates from the eighteenth century.

A maritime theme
Neptune and Britannia feature alongside the coat of arms above the front doorway to Trinity House.

Opposite: **Trinity Market**
Trinity Market, built in 1904 with its low ceilings and small stalls, offers a range of foods and goods on a pleasant, human scale.

TRINITY
1904
MARKET

Time-twine
An imaginative street sculpture in Trinity Square records significant moments in Hull's history.

Old light
Historic structures do not just mean buildings, but include features such as this preserved early electric lamp standard outside Holy Trinity Church.

The KINGSTON
Fine Ales & Beers

Early learning
With origins as far back as 1347 and rebuilt in Tudor style in 1578, the Old Grammar School now houses the Hands on History museum. It counts the seventeenth-century poet Andrew Marvel and the early-nineteenth-century emancipationist William Wilberforce among its 'old boys'.

Opposite: **Flamboyant decoration**
The brightly-painted Kingston public house is another of Hull's wedge-shaped buildings, fitting into the triangular shape of a street corner.

The red corner
Complementing the turquoise of the Kingston public house and the imposing Holy Trinity Church, the London and Manchester Warehousemen's building exerts a strong influence on the south-west corner of Trinity Square.

Georgian terrace
Seen through an arched exit from Trinity Square, the cobbled street and gentle curve of these 1770s terraced-houses in Prince Street come as a complete surprise.

The City's 'Cathedral'
Seen from the top of Kingston House, the roof and tower of the medieval Holy Trinity Church contrasts with the modern shapes of the River Hull tidal surge barrage and The Deep, emphasising the continuing evolution of the city.

Old bricks – large building

With its origins in the late thirteenth century, Holy Trinity Church – one of the largest parish churches in the country – fulfils the architectural role of a cathedral for the city. It is the oldest brick building in England still used for its original purpose, though stone was also used in its construction.

The nave and west window, Holy Trinity Church
For such a large church, the internal structure is surprisingly slender and the atmosphere, bright, colourful and uplifting.

East end, Holy Trinity Church
The original medieval east windows were destroyed during a First World War Zeppelin raid.

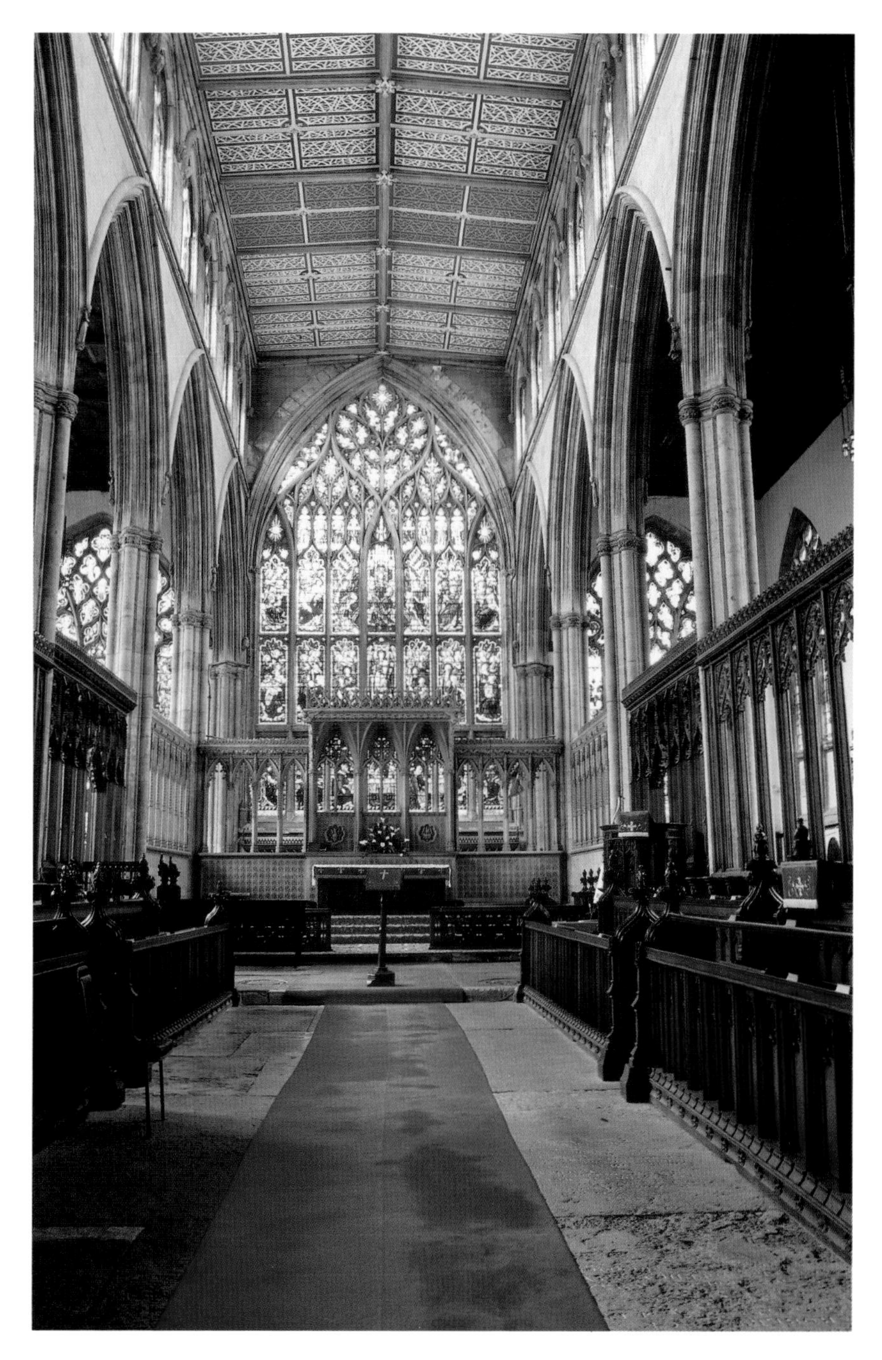

The Font – Holy Trinity Church
William Wilberforce was baptised in Holy Trinity's font, seen here decorated for Easter.

Fixed in time and memory – Holy Trinity Church
The alabaster effigies lying in a niche to the south side of the choir are of Sir William de la Pole and his wife Katherine Norwich, who died in 1366 and 1381 respectively.

Spreading the word – Holy Trinity Church

In the past, it was held that the word of the Lord would be readily spread to all corners of the earth on the back of an eagle, a regal bird, hence the use of the eagle as a lectern. A carved pew end in the choir also includes birds.

A world apart – Holy Trinity Church
Reached by a stone spiral staircase, the bell-ringing chamber set in the tower is a unique, light and airy place. Also housed in the tower is the clock and its workshop and at the top, the bell chamber with a peal of 15 bells.

HOLY TRINITY CHURCH RESTORATION
1899 – 1900.

RESTORATION COMMITTEE FORMED
OCTR 31ST 1898.

P. T. CROOK. MAYOR,– CHAIRMAN,
H. WHITTICK. SHERIFF.

WORK EXECUTED

CHURCH CLEANED, DECORATED & RESTORED,
ELECTRIC LIGHT, NEW HEATING APPARATUS, ORGAN
IMPROVED & ENLARGED, NEW PEAL OF TEN BELLS.

J. HUGHES-GAMES. D.C.L. VICAR.
W. H. WELLSTED. J.P. } CHURCHWARDENS.
C. R. MOXON.

Opposite: **Marks in time – Holy Trinity Church**
Tablets set around the walls of the bell-ringing chamber recount memorable peals (top) and the important Victorian restoration of the church (bottom).

Hepworth's Arcade
Leaving Lowgate behind and entering this Victorian arcade, built in 1894 for the Leeds tailor of that name, you feel like you are taking a step back to another time.

Hull's oldest
St Mary's Church, completed by 1333 and rebuilt over the next two centuries, is Hull's oldest church. It was heavily restored in the 1860s, at which time the base of the tower was cut through to create a footway. Like Holy Trinity, it has benefited recently from restoration works funded by the Heritage Lottery Fund.

Opposite: **Seat of Justice**
The distinctive modern domes of Hull's Combined Court Centre sit surprisingly well with St Mary's Church and the nearby Guildhall and old General Post Office.

COMBINED COURT CENTRE

Seat of power
The east end of the present Guildhall replaced an equally fabulous mid-Victorian town hall. The cupola (top of the tower) of the old Town Hall was preserved and relocated to Pearson Park in the north of the city.

Time on his hands

David Stipetic, the City's clock custodian (left), with the Guildhall clock which he restored and maintains. The clock, in the tower of the Guildhall (right) is just one of several hundred civic clocks which David looks after, so it can truly be said that he has a grip on the beat and rhythm of Hull, for if the clocks are wrong or stop, everyone can become confused.

Victorian delight
Hull is well-served with fine parks such as Pearson Park, which was provided in 1860 by Zachariah Charles Pearson to mark his first term as Mayor. Between 1956 and 1974 the renowned poet Philip Larkin lived in a house overlooking the park.

Civic survival
The demolished Victorian Town Hall (described on page 66) lives on, in part at least, as an unusual historic feature in Pearson Park.

Post past
The old General Post Office forms another stunning contribution to the wealth of architectural interest concentrated at the intersection of Lowgate and Alfred Gelder Street.

Civic pride and confidence

The sheer scale of the Edwardian Guildhall with its powerful roof sculptures, built in response to Hull attaining city status in 1897, emphatically reminds us of the past wealth of the city. Its interior is equally dramatic.

Spirit of the city

Entitled 'Strength', which depicts Britannia riding a chariot flanked by lions (left), and 'Maritime Prowess', which shows Aphrodite in a boat drawn by horses rising from the waves (right), the Guildhall roof sculptures are iconic symbols of Hull.

Mayorial splendour
The Lord Mayor's Parlour, richly decorated with panelling and seventeenth-century-style wood carvings which include fruit and fish, symbols of the city's maritime and trading interests. In front of the long-case clock from the old Town Hall is a framed Hull FC Rugby shirt signed by the players following their success in winning the Rugby League Challenge Cup.

The Council Chamber
Few local politicians in this country will ever experience conducting their business in such a sumptuous setting as Hull's Guildhall.

The necessities of life

Renowned for its fine Victorian public toilets (above left), Hull's modern loos aren't half bad either, as seen here near Queen's Gardens (left) and incorporated into an advertising tower outside the BBC's Media Centre (above).

Where ships once sailed – people now play

Queen's Gardens are a central green lung for the city. They were laid out over the filled-in site of Queen's Dock, Hull's first dock, which was constructed along the line of the moat surrounding the historic city walls in 1778 and closed in 1930.

Hull College

This 1960s' building set across the east end of Queen's Gardens contrasts starkly with the Maritime Museum – the former Docks Offices – at the opposite end of the gardens.

William Wilberforce

The massive stone column built in 1834 to commemorate William Wilberforce, MP, who was responsible for steering through Parliament the abolition of the slave trade in the British Empire, was moved to the east end of Queen's Gardens in front of the modern Hull College, from its original position near the Docks Offices in 1935.

New build

A new building for Hull College embodies the shape of other wedge-shaped buildings in the city... or perhaps it's meant to symbolise the bows of a ship ... or neither?

A haven of calm

Take time to linger in Kingston Square (above), a charming frontispiece to the Hull New Theatre. On the west side, the façade of the old Hull and East Riding School of Medicine and Anatomy, built in 1831, is now clutched in the embrace of a modern development (left). Ghastly violation or imaginative evolution? What do you think?

An evening out
Hull New Theatre's imposing exterior is matched by its recently-refurbished interior. Built in the 1830s, the modern redecoration has followed the colour themes of that time.

Enjoy the style
Relish the comfortable auditorium and the theatre's delightful circle lounge, with its unique view over Kingston Square.

Follow the fish – experience the city
An imaginative *Seven Seas* Fish Trail leads from City Hall, where you can buy a trail guide, through the Old Town to the museums and other sites. Different species of fish are depicted in panels as way-markers set into the pavements.

Little left
Remains of the old city walls built of brick in the 1320s, the most extensive use of this material in medieval England, at Beverley Gate, one of the four main entrances to the historic walled town.

Opposite: **Ghost walls**
Coloured bricks set into the pavements are used to trace the route of the old town walls down Princes Dock and Humber Dock Streets.

The Deep & Museums

Old meets new, or new meets old?
The old Princes Dock and Princes Quay shopping centre walkway, backed by the Maritime Museum, sum up both the heritage and modern vitality of the city.

Opposite: **Shop over the dock**
Princes Quay, a modern shopping centre on four floors, stands on stilts over the old Princes Dock.

Trinity House
Opposite Princes Quay, several attractive buildings form the western frontage of Trinity House, such as Roland House (left) and the gated entrance to the inner courtyard. (opposite).

1842

An accomplished conversion
These former dock-side warehouses in Princes Dock Street have been sensitively converted to a new use.

Green bricks
Glazed coloured bricks and tiles are a frequent feature of some old buildings, especially public houses, as seen on the rather obviously-named Green Bricks public house in Humber Dock Street.

From work to pleasure
Humber Dock and the adjacent Railway Dock have been converted into a successful and attractive marina.

Night light
Once a key safety feature in the dangerous waters around the mouth of the Humber Estuary at Spurn Point, the Spurn Lightship, built in 1927, is now permanently moored in the marina and is seasonally open to the public.

Quick-turnabout
A small railway turntable for 90-degree changes of direction of wagons has been preserved along with a section of rails on the quayside of the old Humber Dock at the marina.

Fresh face to the river
New offices on the waterfront, set in a wide public plaza, complement the quality of the adjacent riverfront at Victoria Pier.

A nasty surprise
Unwelcome intruders beware. A last line of defence at the entrance to the old Humber Dock.

A unique symbol
In the days of nationalised utilities, only Hull retained its own telephone system. While red telephone boxes were the norm elsewhere, Hull had white.

Overleaf: **Crossing the Humber**
Before the Humber Bridge was built, Victoria Pier was the ferry terminal for crossing the river if you wanted to avoid a 60-mile trip round to the other side of the Humber. The Pier offers a magnificent vantage point from which to watch river life and to view The Deep.

PILOT OFFICE
NELSON STREET
QUEEN STREET

Opposite: **Pathfinders' place**
Now redeveloped, the imposing building of the old Pilots' Office is an important and colourful feature in the character of the area around Victoria Pier.

Energy for the future
An innovative building, sporting photocells and wind turbines to generate electricity, is an eye-catching counterbalance to the heavy traffic using the adjacent Castle Street.

King Billy

The gold-leafed statue of King William III, seen from the top of Holy Trinity Church in a torrential rainstorm, positively glows in the gloom, as well as at ground level next to his eponymous pub on a fine day (above right). The statue is affectionately known locally as 'King Billy.'

Harbour link
Bishop Lane links across High Street to Bishop Staith, one of the historic routes by which goods would have been transported to and from ships in port in the Old Harbour along the River Hull.

Dated delivery
Initial letters on old post boxes denote the monarch in whose reign the box was installed. VR stands for Victoria Regina – so this post box in High Street has been receiving letters for more than a century.

Time-honoured politician
Wilberforce House, an Elizabethan mansion and the nineteenth-century home of the famous MP, is a highlight of Hull's delightful Museums Quarter. Wilberforce's statue stands in the front garden (above). The house is open to the public.

Calm for contemplation
The tranquillity of Wilberforce House rear garden and the adjacent Nelson Mandela and Mahatma Ghandi Gardens are places for quiet reflection on the enormity of the contributions made by these individuals to humankind.

Celebrating citizens

The city of Hull has a long tradition of honouring the great and the good whom it holds in high regard. William de la Pole – the first Mayor of Hull (left); Andrew Marvel – poet (centre); and Amy Johnson – aviator (right), are just some of the people permanently remembered.

Streetlife and quality of life
A bust of Mahatma Ghandi watches over the pretty Ghandi Gardens, outside the Streetlife Museum, home to a large collection telling the story of transport over the last two centuries.

A snapshot in time
The main street in the Streetlife Museum includes shops of yesteryear and a dizzily low-flying historic aeroplane.

Streetlife on rails
Trams – why did we get rid of them? A beautiful example.

Decay and renewal
Thoughtfully, these old petrol pumps have been left worn and faded, just like they were when in use (left); while the radiator of the museum's Morris Commercial van shows that the vehicle has been restored to pristine condition (above).

Travel through time
The exceptional Hull and East Riding Museum, to the south of Mahatma Ghandi Gardens, presents a concise and highly enjoyable picture of local life through the ages.

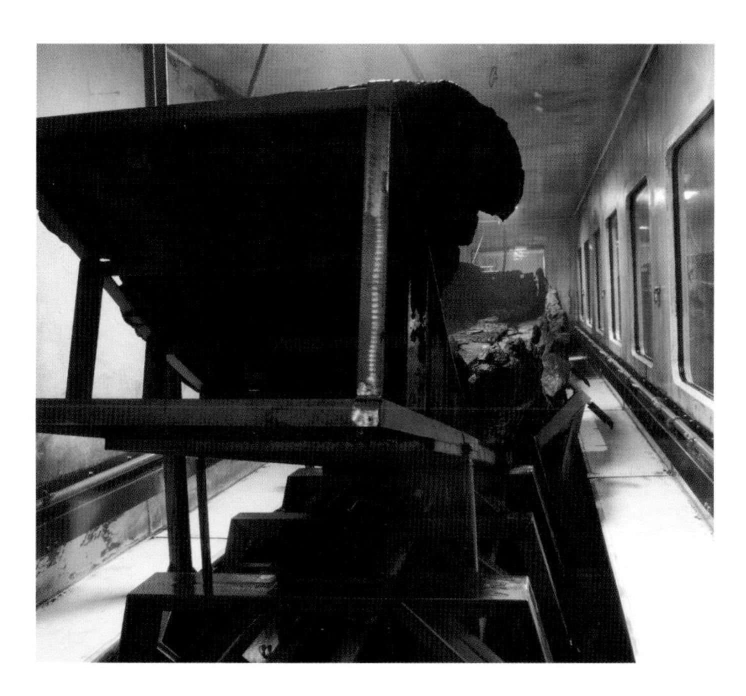

People in the past
One of the enigmatic and haunting Roos Carr figures (right), 2600 years old, (watching me… watching him…watching me), possesses a power similar to the carved stone heads of Easter Island; while the awesome, only 300 years younger, Hasholme boat (above), carved from a single 45-feet/14m long oak tree trunk, is undergoing a lengthy conservation process in a special chamber.

Last of a line
The *Arctic Corsair* (a sidewinder trawler), one of the exhibits in the Museums Quarter, is a tangible reminder of the city's fishing heritage.

Opposite: **Keeping the tide at bay**
The tidal surge barrage straddling the River Hull is lowered in times of high flood risk to protect the city.

Decaying dry-dock
Lying alongside the mouth of the River Hull, this dock's working life is over. But as an historic listed building, the dock structure has to be protected as part any redevelopment plans. What will its future hold?

River traffic

Barges, used to transport goods locally along the Humber, at their mooring on the River Hull, in an area proposed for re-development. International shipping is now concentrated in the docks to the east of the city and the other Humber ports.

Economics rule

The economic role of many of the large mills along the River Hull has now past, leaving huge buildings for which new viable commercial and industrial uses are not easily found.

Bridge-spotters' paradise
For those keen on bridges, the River Hull offers an unusual array. Drypool Bridge is a steel bascule bridge which rocks back to open with the aid of a counter-balancing weight.

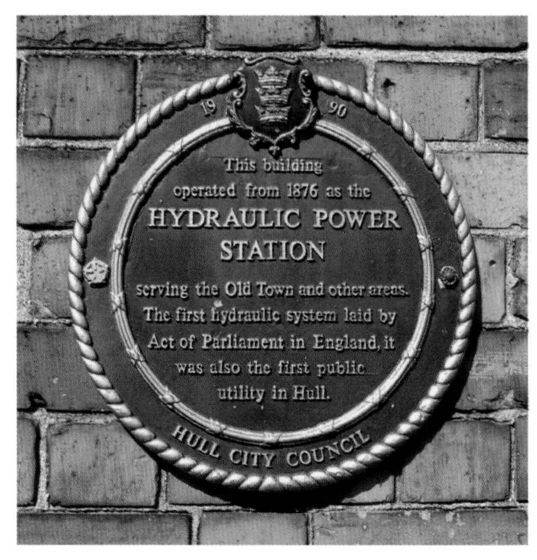

First power
The extraordinary 1876 Hydraulic Power Station, with a large water tank on its roof, was the first such facility in any city. One of Hull's blue Heritage Plaques records its importance.

Heavenly houses
Turning from the Wincolmlee into Charterhouse Lane, you cannot fail but be impressed by a pair of lovely buildings facing each other in otherwise largely unexceptional surroundings. They are Charterhouse (above) and the house where the seventeenth-century poet Andrew Marvel lived when his father was Master at Charterhouse (right).

Industrial construction
North Bridge is another bascule bridge, fronted by a solid concrete construction. The bridge has a curious aside in the form of an old bank building, suggesting greater wealth in this area in the past.

Bridge over nothing
New Cleveland Street Bridge, the first to be built in this country using a special ferro-concrete method in 1902, today bridges nothing, but its structure remains. An inscribed plaque on one of its pillars records its origins.

Stuck up
By-passed by other routes across the River Hull, Scott Street Bridge remains in the open position due to the failure of its water hydraulic mechanism.

Opposite: **Railway bridge with no trains**
Wilmington Swing Bridge once carried the railway from Hull to Victoria Docks and to the seaside towns of Withernsea and Hornsea. It finally closed as a rail route in 1968, and today provides a cycle and pedestrian crossing of the River Hull.

WILMINGTON
BRIDGE

In the eye of the beholder?
While not conventionally attractive, these massive commercial buildings nevertheless do have a certain functional charm.

The Deep
Emerging from the fog across the mouth of the River Hull, the world's only submarium has given Hull a new modern focus, similar, but on an obviously smaller scale, to the role Sydney's Opera House plays for that city.

Overleaf: **Magnetic shore**
Standing close to the site of the Citadel, part of Hull's historic eastern defences demolished in the mid nineteenth century to make way for Victoria Dock, The Deep attracts thousands of visitors each year.

Symbol of acquatic supremacy
A shark sculpture (above) on the waterfront hints at the subjects to be seen in The Deep's exhibit of world-wide marine habitats (left).

Colour and coral
Varied fish and other animals present a vivid picture of life in tropical seas.

Close encounters
Vast tanks, faced with floor-to-ceiling glass, create the illusion that you are actually under the sea with the fish.

Opposite: **From Castle, to dock, to housing estate**
Built where Henry VIII's fortress once stood, Victoria Dock's usefulness passed and much of the dock was filled in and turned into desirable housing, complete with a promenade along the Humber.

All that remains
A small part of the fortress which formed the city's medieval defences survived and was moved to a site in Victoria Dock (above), where an old pump-house (top right) and a basin (right) from the Dockland era have also been preserved.

Centre of trade
The Port of Hull, along with sister ports of Immingham and Goole, is among the most thriving ports in the UK. More than 4000 ships dock in Hull each year.

Overleaf: **Gateway to Europe**
P&O's North Sea Ferries are a popular way to travel to the Continent. They are also a vital link in the E8 Trans-Pennine/Trans-Europe walking and cycling trail from Ireland to Istanbul.

P&O Ferries
ABP PORT OF HULL

P&O

Tough guys
Small but powerful tugs are used to manoeuvre ships and barges (left). A similarly strong machine, an 1885 steam crane capable of lifting 100 tons, is protected in retirement as an historic listed building (above). It looks, almost sadly, across the docks at its modern counterparts picking up much smaller loads.

Part of the scene

The large, slab-sided ferries – *The Pride of Bruges* shown here is a smaller one – remain in port most of the daylight hours, and as such seem as permanent a feature in the riverscape as large buildings.

Top deck

The helicopter pad atop the massive *Pride of Hull* on a stunningly beautiful and hot day presents quite a surreal appearance.

Ship and city – it's all in the name

The *Pride of Hull,* one of the largest ferries in the world, loading for her voyage to Rotterdam on a late spring afternoon.

Opposite: **City limits**
The cooling towers of BP's Salt End chemical works behind a field of rape near Paull.

Closing mark
The diminutive old Paull Lighthouse, built in 1836 by Trinity House on a sharp bend in the River Humber, represents the closing 'quotation mark' at the end of our journey.

Reverse view

The distance to the Humber Bridge, 10 miles (16 kms) from Paull, reminds us of the scale and variety of interest Hull and this notable stretch of the Humber waterfront has to offer for those prepared to seek it out and pause a while to enjoy it.